Contents

The elephant

The elephant has a huge, grey body and strong legs that look like pillars. It has a long **trunk** instead of the short nose that we humans have. It also has large, flapping ears. Most elephants have **tusks**, which are extra-long teeth either side of their trunk. Male elephants are called bulls and females are called cows.

A fully grown female elephant uses her trunk to feed on grass.

4

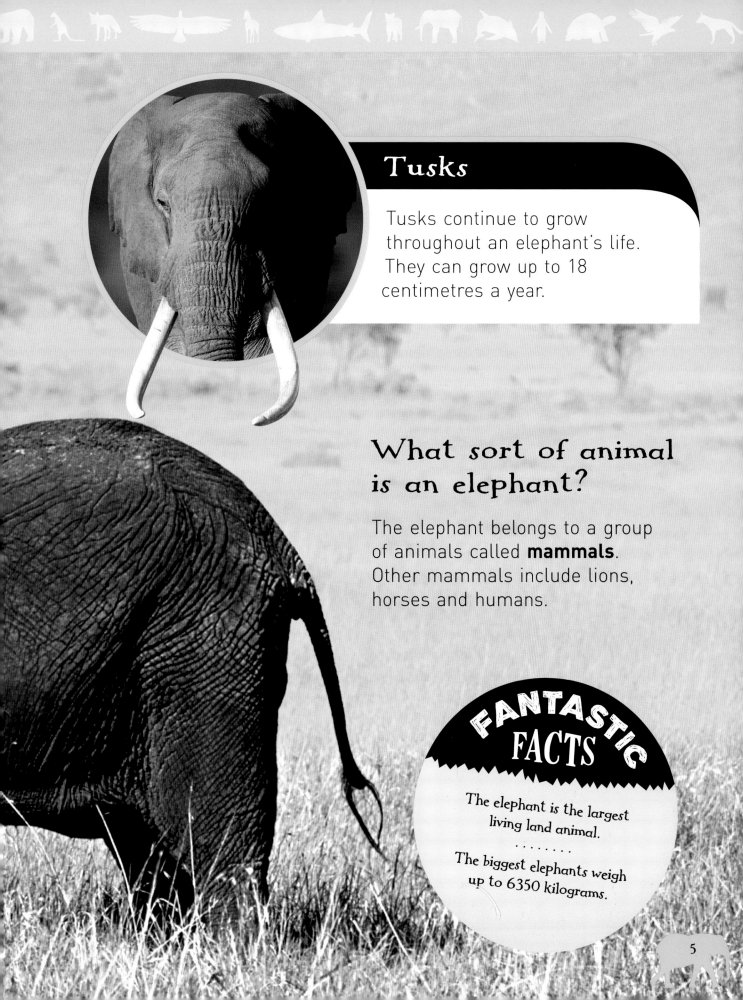

Tusks

Tusks continue to grow throughout an elephant's life. They can grow up to 18 centimetres a year.

What sort of animal is an elephant?

The elephant belongs to a group of animals called **mammals**. Other mammals include lions, horses and humans.

FANTASTIC FACTS

The elephant is the largest living land animal.
. . . .
The biggest elephants weigh up to 6350 kilograms.

Elephant types

There are three species, or types, of elephant. They are the African, African forest and Asian elephants. The Asian elephant is often called the Indian elephant. Look quickly and you may think the African and African forest elephants appear the same, but there are differences between all three species.

FANTASTIC FACT

Male and female African elephants both have tusks, but only the male Asian elephant has them.
. . . .
The African elephant has a dip in its back. The Asian elephant has an arched back.

Asian elephant

The Asian elephant is the smallest species of elephant. It has small ears and a long face. Its skin is less wrinkly than that of African elephants.

African elephant

The African elephant is the largest of the elephants. It has large ears, long tusks and wrinkly skin.

African elephants have very large ears.

African forest elephant

The African forest elephant is smaller than its cousin the African elephant. It also has a hairy trunk. Its tusks point downwards so they do not get tangled up in forest **vegetation**.

Where elephants live

The African elephant is found mainly in East Africa, on tropical grassland known as **savanna**. The savanna is a vast, open plain covered in grass and a few trees. The African forest elephant is found in the forests of Central and West Africa. The Asian elephant lives across South and Southeast Asia.

FANTASTIC FACT

The African forest elephant is difficult to spot in its dense forest home. This means we know less about it than about African and Asian elephants.

African forest elephants live in thick, tropical forests.

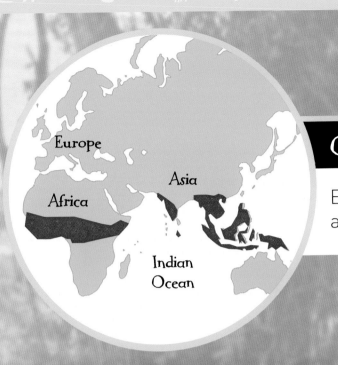

Europe

Asia

Africa

Indian
Ocean

On the map

Elephants are found in the areas shown in pink.

Asian elephant

The Asian elephant lives on grassland and in forests. It has become domesticated, which means it has been captured and kept by humans for thousands of years. Asian elephants can be trained to do jobs such as carrying passengers or lifting heavy logs. An adult elephant can drag about half its own weight.

Beginning life

After mating with a bull elephant, a female elephant is **pregnant** for 22 months. She gives birth to only one baby at a time. A baby elephant is called a calf. A newborn calf has reddish hair over its head and back. It gradually loses this hair as it gets older.

FANTASTIC FACT

A newborn elephant calf weighs between 77 and 113 kilograms. It stands almost 90 centimetres high from the ground to its shoulder.

Starting a family

A female elephant is old enough to have a calf when she is about 17 years old. She will have six or seven calves during her lifetime. Females stop mating when they reach about 50 years of age.

Calves

Elephant calves feed on their mothers' milk, drinking up to 11 litres of milk every day. Calves have lots to take in. They must learn how to use their trunks and how to behave around the adult members of the herd.

Female elephants touch their calves a lot.

A special day

The birth of a baby elephant is a special day for the herd. All the elephants crowd around the mother to touch her new calf. The elephants are very excited and make a lot of noise.

Growing up

A female elephant usually has several youngsters with her, ranging in age from a few months to ten years. Young calves are protected by the herd. If the mother dies, the other elephants look after her young.

Young elephants stay with their mother for between eight and ten years.

Changing diet

The calf becomes an **adolescent** once it stops drinking its mother's milk at about three years of age. By this time it has teeth, which means it can eat plant food.

Getting bigger

Female elephants keep growing until they are about 20 years old. They do not grow much after this. Bull elephants, however, continue to grow until they are about 30 years old.

FANTASTIC FACTS

An African elephant weighs about 1000 kilograms by the time it is six years old.

· · · · · · · ·

About half of all elephants die before they reach the age of 15.

13

Living in a herd

Female elephants live in family groups called herds. A typical herd is made up of three or four adult females and their calves. All the adult females are related. The herd is led by the oldest female, called the matriarch. The herd gets larger as more calves are born, so some of the females may leave and form their own herd.

Young elephants learn by watching their mothers and the other members of the herd.

Bull elephants

The young bulls in the herd all play together. They charge at each other and make a lot of noise. When they leave the herd, they live on their own or join other males. The adult bulls only rejoin the herd when a female is ready to mate. Then they go off on their own again.

FANTASTIC FACT

Sometimes herds join up to form a large family group that may have more than 200 elephants in it.

Feeding

Elephants are plant eaters, or herbivores. They use their long trunks to reach up into the trees for leaves or fruit, or to pick grass from the ground. Elephants also use their sturdy tusks to dig for roots in the ground and to pull down trees.

Growing tusks

By the time they are three years old, calves can eat plants. As they grow older, calves learn to use their trunks for finding food. They also learn what is good to eat and what they should avoid. Adults in the herd help the younger elephants feed by pulling down branches for them.

What do elephants eat?

During the rainy months, elephants eat mostly grass. During the dry months, they eat shrubs, twigs and bark. They eat flowers, fruits and roots all year round.

Elephants can stand on their back legs and stretch up with their trunks to reach the highest branches.

FANTASTIC FACT

Every day, an adult elephant eats more than 150 kilograms of food — that is the combined weight of two men!

Teeth

Elephants use their teeth for grinding plant food. They break the food down into small pieces and then they swallow it. Calves are born with four large teeth that are flat. New teeth form in the back of the mouth and push the old ones out.

FANTASTIC FACT

An elephant's tooth is the largest tooth of any mammal.
. . . .
Adult elephants have 26 teeth, including two tusks.

Adult teeth

An elephant usually grows six sets of teeth in its lifetime. The final set appear when it is about 40 years old. These are the largest set — each tooth is 21 centimetres long and weighs almost 4 kilograms! An elephant's teeth wear down as it gets older.

Growing tusks

A tusk grows from a tooth at the front of the elephant's mouth. It is made of **ivory**. Calves have tiny baby tusks, which drop out and are replaced by permanent tusks.

An elephant moves its jaws from side to side, grinding leaves between its teeth.

Trunks

The trunk is formed from the elephant's nose and upper lip. There are two nostrils that run down the whole trunk. Elephants use their trunks for breathing, smelling, picking things up and trumpeting. The end of the trunk is very sensitive to touch. It has finger-like flaps at the end.

Elephants rely on their trunks to sense danger in the air.

Smell

Smell helps to keep the herd together. It allows elephants to detect predators such as lions or tigers. At the first hint of danger, an elephant raises its trunk to smell the air. Smell also helps elephants find food and water.

Using their trunks

Elephants can pick up small objects with the end of their trunks in the same way that we use our fingertips. Calves learn to use their trunks, just like human babies learn to walk. The calf learns how to use the different muscles to control movement.

FANTASTIC FACT

The trunk plays such an important part in an elephant's life that it is almost impossible for an elephant to survive if its trunk is damaged.

21

Communication

Elephants communicate with each other through sound, touch and gestures. They make a trumpeting sound with their trunks when they are excited, surprised or when they are about to attack. They also squeal, cry, scream, roar, snort and groan! Elephants use deep rumbling sounds, too low for us to hear. These can be heard by other elephants as far as 9 kilometres away.

FANTASTIC FACT

Elephants use more than 70 kinds of sounds and 160 different signals in their daily lives. Most 'elephant talk' takes place during the afternoon.

Adult signals

Grown-up elephants flap their ears or raise their trunks and tails to communicate with each other. These are warnings to other animals that the elephant is angry. Touch is important, too. Elephants of all ages touch each other with their trunks when they meet.

Learning to trumpet

As they get older, calves learn to make all the sounds that elephant adults use to communicate. As their bodies get bigger and their trunks get longer, young elephants are able to make louder sounds.

Elephants use signals such as a raised trunk to show anger.

23

Moving

Elephants are such large animals that they need a big, strong skeleton to support their body. Muscles wrap around and attach to the bones. When the muscles **contract**, they pull on the bone to make it move.

Walking, running — and sliding!

Elephants can walk and run, but they can't leap or jump like many other mammals. They walk at speeds of up to 13 kilometres per hour. To walk faster they take longer, quicker strides. Sometimes elephants climb up slopes or slide down them.

FANTASTIC FACT

Elephants can walk almost silently because they have a spongy cushion on the bottom of their feet, which muffles any noise.

Charge!

A charging elephant runs at 40 kilometres per hour — that's much faster than a human can run.

A herd of elephants can walk 80 kilometres in a day.

Keeping cool

Elephants live in hot climates. Their large bodies heat up in the sun, so they often need to cool down. One way they do this is by visiting water holes or rivers and having a swim. Elephants spend hours resting by water. The calves like to throw water over each other. Elephants love to wallow in mud, too. A covering of mud helps protect their skin. It acts like sunblock, which is what we use to protect our skin from the sun.

FANTASTIC FACT

Elephants flap their ears to stay cool. The flapping motion allows them to lose heat to the surrounding air.

Elephants keep cool by spraying water over themselves with their trunks.

Finding shade

During the hottest part of the day, elephants stand in the shade to stay cool. An elephant calf's skin is very sensitive to the sun. The mother elephant stands over her calves and young to shade them. As an elephant gets older, its skin gets thicker.

Elephants in danger

Sadly, the number of elephants in the world has fallen. Many African elephants have been killed by humans for their ivory tusks. Today, most elephants are protected and live in national parks. These are places where the elephants cannot be harmed. Tourists can drive around the parks and see the elephants.

You can go on safari to see elephants in Africa's national parks.

Disappearing homes

Elephants are suffering because their **habitat** is being damaged. Forest trees are cut down for timber. Grasslands are used for grazing cattle and growing crops. This means there is less food and space for the elephants to live in.

Ivory

Ivory is valuable to humans. It is used to make ornaments and jewellery. During the 1970s and 1980s, thousands of elephants were killed. In 1989, there was a ban on the sale of ivory.

FANTASTIC FACT

There are about 600,000 African elephants and 50,000 Asian elephants in the world.

29

Life cycle of an elephant

A female elephant is pregnant for 22 months. She gives birth to a single calf. Young elephants drink their mothers' milk for three years. They stay close to their mother for 10 years. Young males leave the herd once they reach 13 to 15 years of age. The female elephants stay with the herd. Elephants live to about 70 years of age.

calf

older calf

adult

Glossary

adolescent the stage in growing up between childhood and adulthood

contract to get shorter

habitat the place where an animal, or a plant lives

ivory the hard white substance that makes up the tusk of an elephant

mammal a warm-blooded animal with a backbone. Mammals give birth to live young, rather than laying eggs. The female mammal produces milk for her young

pregnant a female animal that has a baby developing inside her

savanna a grassy plain with a few trees, found in tropical parts of the world, for example East and Southern Africa

trunk the very long nose of an elephant

tusk a long pointed tooth that sticks out of an elephant's mouth

vegetation plant life

Index